UNDER THE WHITE WING
EVENTS AT SAND CREEK

ALSO BY CHARLES L. SQUIER

The Sonnet: A Comprehensive Anthology of British and American Sonnets
(with R.M. Bender), 1965
Sir John Suckling, 1978
John Fletcher, 1986

Poetry Chapbooks

Mrs. Beeton's Tea Party, 1995
Monday, Wednesday, Friday at Ten, 2005

With [illegible] memories [illegible] best wishes,

CHARLES SQUIER

UNDER THE WHITE WING EVENTS AT SAND CREEK

Cross-Cultural Communications
Merrick, New York
2011

ACKNOWLEDGMENTS

Excerpts of an earlier version of this poem were published as "A Sand Creek
Narrative" in *The Midwest Review*, 3:1, Spring, 1978. I wish to thank the Colorado
Historical Society for permission to quote from the "Unfinished Manuscript" of
Edward W. Wynkoop. Thanks are also given to the Department of English and the
College of Arts and Sciences, University of Colorado at Boulder. The photographs,
scans 100025737 and 10025492, Copyright Colorado Historical Society, are printed
with the permission of the Colorado Historical Society. I have relied on Stan Hoig,
The Sand Creek Massacre (Norman, Oklahoma, 1961) and Duane Schultz, *Month
of the Freezing Moon* (New York, 1990) for many historical details. Thom Hatch's
Black Kettle: The Cheyenne Chief Who Sought Peace but Found War (Hoboken,
New Jersey, 2004) provided an excellent account of the Sand Creek Massacre, its
historical context, as well as the life of a central historical actor. I also consulted
web based sites and note in particular the National Park Service's http://www.nps.
gov/sand/ and its links.

Editor-Publisher: **Stanley H. Barkan**

Published in the United States by
Cross-Cultural Communications
239 Wynsum Avenue
Merrick, NY 11566-4725
Tel: (516) 868-5636 / Fax: (516) 379-1901
Email: cccpoetry@aol.com
www.cross-culturalcommunications.com

Library of Congress Control Number: 2010941371

Cloth Edition/ISBN 978-0-89304-541-8
Paperback Edition/ISBN 978-0-89304-542-5

Front cover illustration by Chuck Squier
Back cover photo by Jan Squier

Designed by Tchouki
Hardcover by Frank Papp
Printed in Bulgaria

for Jan, Alison, Chuck,
and the memory of Nina La Barge Squier
for whom the past was always present

Arrival of Chiefs in Denver (*Courtesy Colorado Historical Society*)

PREFACE

In the early morning of November 29, 1864, a force of some seven hundred soldiers, comprised of units of the First and Third Colorado Volunteer Regiments under the command of Colonel John M. Chivington, a Methodist preacher turned soldier, attacked a camp of Cheyenne and Arapahoe Indians situated on a bend of Sand Creek, in eastern Colorado, north of the present-day town of Lamar. There were approximately one hundred lodges of Indians, about two hundred men and five hundred women and children, made up of the bands of Black Kettle, War Bonnet, White Antelope, Lone Bear, Left Hand, and Sand Hill.

The Indians were under the impression that they were at peace with the Whites and under the protection of Major Scott J. Anthony, the commanding officer of Fort Lyon some forty miles to the southwest. Black Kettle and other chiefs had met with Major Wynkoop, Governor Evans of the Territory of Colorado, and Colonel Chivington at Camp Weld, near Denver, in September. Although the conference at Fort Weld arrived at no specific agreements, it left the Indians with the belief that they would be safe in their winter camp at Sand Creek.

Colonel Chivington clearly shared no such view and began preparations to attack Black Kettle's Indians. Chivington, rabidly anti-Indian and pro-settler, believed that the only way to peace in the Indian country was through the extermination of the Indians.

The Indians at Sand Creek were caught by surprise and at least one hundred fifty were killed. Chivington claimed over five hundred killed. Most of the dead were women and children. All of the Indian dead were scalped, and many were otherwise mutilated. The Colorado Third, with its collection of scalps, returned to Denver to be greeted with wild popular acclaim; however, when the news of the massacre reached the national press, revulsion over the massacre grew. Military and Congressional investigations followed. Chivington was staunchly defended by his supporters, especially by the former members of the Colorado Third, but his reputation and that of the Colorado Third were both destroyed. The immediate consequence of the massacre at Sand Creek was the escalation of White and Indian violence along the Platte. In longer historical terms the massacre at Sand Creek exemplifies the deceit, betrayal and genocide, which characterized so much of the "winning of the West."

7

Black Kettle and the Chiefs, Denver, 1864. Black Kettle, center with Peace pipe. White Antelope is at his far right; Neva is between them. Bull Bear is to Black Kettle's left. Wynkoop and Soule kneel in front. John Smith is third from the left in the back. *(Courtesy Colorado Historical Society)*

I. Prelude

First the landscape—treeless, barren.
Snow-drifted prairie in early dawn,
Then cue in sound:
Horses—whinnies and snorts,
Steady hoof falls and rattle of gear,
Cavalry on the move.
Now, let the camera show the line
Trotting in columns of four,
The companies with their flags and guidons,
The four twelve-pound mountain howitzers,
Supply and ambulance wagons,
A long shot, some seven hundred men,
In five battalions riding.
Superimpose caption,
COLORADO TERRITORY, NOVEMBER 29, 1864.
Bugle calls, "Gallop,"
Now swell in theme.
All familiar.
The troops gallop beneath the title,
EVENTS AT SAND CREEK
Starring whomever you want as
John M. Chivington, Colonel Commanding,
First Colorado District and First Indian Expedition.
Close-up, massive Chivington,
Stern, cold-eyed,
An eagle, a lion, certified hero
Any time or place,
"Finest figure of a military man I ever saw."
Pastor Chivington preaching in a rough saloon
In a raw town.
The bartender would come to church,
The gamblers and pimps tip their hats.
And he had style, not just the looks.
Back there in that little church in St. Joe,
He preached the Free Soil Word,
Thundered to slavery threats,
"Tar and feather me, silence me?

9

Silence God's voice? Oh, no.
I mean to preach by His grace . . ."
Grace thundered to shake the walls,
Pause, emphatic silence, buzz of flies,
Thunder again,
"And by these two pistols here,
 By this Bible, let us pray."
Through the little towns,
Tough frontier stations,
He preached the Word.
After he arrived ladies could walk the streets,
The whores stayed out of sight.
The Presiding Elders knew their man
Rough diamond, that chap,
Move him on with the frontier,
Follow him up with preachers with clean nails,
At ease in drawing rooms,
Comfortable with harmoniums and even Emerson.
Missouri, Kansas, then, Colorado,
Riding out from Denver to preach the Word
In Hamilton, Buckskin Joe, Georgia Gulch.
"Hear the Preacher, George?"
"Yeah, big tough son of a bitch, ain't he?"
He attacked Mammon
And reported a "profitable season of worship"
When he preached in the saloon in Idaho Springs.
Arapahoe, Cheyenne, Ute watched as the trails
Pushed through the buffalo lands towards gold,
Gold, in the streams clear as gin,
Gold, sweated out of dark holes.
And after the miners, came the farmers and their families.
"May the Lord bless you and keep you,
May the Lord cause His face to smile down upon you
And give you peace this day and evermore."
"Amen, brother."
"Mason, too, Big John,"
"Oh. yes, Grand Master of Colorado."
"Sits a horse well, don't he?"
"Busts up too many whorehouses for my money.
But I won't cross the big bastard . . ."

Still on Chivington this long freeze-frame.
Now here dissolve through Chivington's eyes
To Chivington at Glorieta Pass, New Mexico Territory,
1862 and his First Colorado Volunteers
Slamming down on the Confederate flank.
Chivington surveys it all,
The Rebel wagons burn,
General Sibley's advance stopped dead.
Chivington's great victory in New Mexico
Ends Confederate hopes in the west,
Trumpets *The Rocky Mountain News.*
"The Union forever, hurrah, boys, hurrah!"
Dusty Larimer Street in Denver,
Tambien Saloon, a director's dream, authentic West,
"Goddamn! Old Chivington showed the Rebs!
Son of a bitch, he's something for a preacher."
"Have a drink on that."
"I don't mind, Colorado, the Union, and Chivington!"
What bells there are ring out over the little town.
Pastor Chivington, muscular Christian, declares
"Governor Gilpin, I thank you,
But I've preached the word of God in peace,
Now, in war I must bear His Sword of Righteousness
No chaplaincy, give me a fighting commission in the First,
I ride with the God of Battles now."

Chivington filled the room,
That sort of man, presence, bulk,
Assassin's eyes and an ad man's smile,
Package that, you've got the sale,
Better, power.
Oh, tough and genial.
"Pastor was so kind,"
Mrs. Norton, looking up from her needles
At the quilting says,
"So kind."
Mary Jean, sixteen, says nothing,
Remembers when he preached,
Towering gentle, "God in His gentleness,
"Forgives," he said, gentle,

His voice, soft, deep, gentle;
"But," rising now, deep, a thunder,
"In his wrath, sinners, destroys."
Mary Jean drowsing in the early light,
Just hearing the roosters
And dreaming of John Chivington,
Not handsome, but so powerful and strong,
Dreaming before she rises to light the fire.
The red dawn seeps out of Kansas Territory,
Mary Jane shudders, remembering the Hungates,
All murdered and the mother raped, they said.
The little girls chopped to bits.
Arapahoe and Cheyenne lurking somewhere in that red light.
Imagine being thrown over the pony's neck,
In the smoke and fire, Denver City burning.
It could happen.
Roman Nose could come.
And then on buffalo hide in the smoky lodge,
Thrust and tear, sweat, smell of hides,
The one-eyed Indian on Larimer Street.
Laura Roper was captured. What happened to her?
Mrs. Snyder hanged herself.
But Chivington would . . .
"Mary Jean, get up!"
Mary Jean quilts, smiles.
That was 1864.
 Mary Jean quilting in 1924 still remembered,
"Oh, yes, I remember Colonel Chivington,
He was our pastor for a while,
I was just a girl then,
But I remember his sermons.
He spoke very well."

* * *

Chivington's troops move on,
Dismounted now, leading the horses.
Walk, trot, gallop, dismount and lead;
Cavalry discipline holds even the new, raw men,
The Hundreddazers, Colorado Third.

"Why, they almost look like soldiers," says Captain Soule,
Commanding officer, Company D, First Colorado Volunteers,
Soule, the Jayhawk daredevil, might have saved
John Brown's men, had they wanted to be saved,
From that West Virginia jail and the hangman's rope.
"Colonel, I tell you and this is true,
There are no hostiles at Sand Creek.
Those Indians are there at Major Wynkoop's word.
They just want peace;
They've come in. You were at Camp Weld,
Colonel, you know what Black Kettle said."
"Captain, damn any man in sympathy with an Indian."
"Mount. Troop, forward, walk!"
Cavalry moves on over the prairie,
Stars seem brighter for the cold,
Patches of snow gleam.
Chivington thinks of reputation and reports,
A heroic march, maybe Joshua,
But no snow there.
"Sir, I have the honor to report,"
And certainly a telegram to Byers at *The Rocky Mountain News*,
But later for that.

> *In some instances they have attacked and killed*
> *soldiers and murdered peaceable citizens. For*
> *this the Great Father is angry, and will certainly*
> *hunt them out and punish them, but he does not want*
> *to hurt those who remain friendly to the whites.*
> *He desires to protect and take care of them. For*
> *this purpose I direct that all friendly Indians*
> *keep away from those who are at war, and go to*
> *places of safety. Friendly Arapahoes and Cheyennes*
> *belonging on the Arkansas River will go to Major*
> *Colley, U.S. Indian agent at Fort Lyon who will give*
> *them provisions and show them a place of safety . . .*
> *The object of this is to prevent friendly Indians*
> *From being killed by mistake.*

June 27, 1864, Governor Evans by Proclamation
Does not wish
In the Territory of Colorado
Friendly Indians
To be killed
By mistake.
By Proclamation,
John Evans, Governor.

                              * * *

Wind blows over the prairie,
The tall grass sways and sighs,
But the buffalo are unhappy.
Black Kettle worries, walks in the night,
Listening to the winds,
Coyotes howl.
Listening, looking for a sign.

Slight wisps of smoke
Still rise from the burned house.
Wind in the grass,
A hawk circles.
On the willow
A redwing blackbird sings.
The children are absolutely still.
There is blood on their blond hair.
Heads being nearly severed,
From their bodies.
The mother is also still now,
Limbs askew, torn, ripped,
An abstraction.
Hungate himself is harder to find,
Down by the stream,
Well, pieces of him.
The waters of Burning Creek
Are cold, clear, and bright.

Be not misled by the flying rumors, and do
not keep your command out longer than there is
prospect of success nor encumber your command
with prisoner Indians.
                    —Chivington, Colonel Commanding

"That stroke I admired,
Encumber your command.
Kill them all.
Murdering redskin heathens,
Godless murderers.
Some of them, two, three wives,
Do what they want
And carry off white women, too.
Use them anyway,
Strip them naked in their tents,
Young blond girls
And those brownskinned squaws.
Remember that whore I saved in Buckskin Joe,
All the miners had her, but beautiful,
Marsy what's her name in St. Joe,
Always smiled, cast down her eyes,
Oh, I was tempted,
Those breasts and rush of hair.
But I didn't fall.
I do God's work now.
What did they do to Mrs. Snyder
To make her hang herself?
Mouthing those white breasts,
Sodom in those tents.
And there were also sodomites in the land and
they did according to all the abominations
of the nations which the lord cast out before
the children of Israel.
Heathen sodomites and worshippers of Baal,
God knows what they worship, witches, witchcraft,

   Thou shalt not suffer a witch to live.
   So Joshua smote all the country of the hills,

and of the south, and of the vale, and of the
springs, and all their kings: He left none
remaining, but utterly destroyed all that breathed,
as the Lord God of Israel commanded.

I've heard His voice in the camps,
In the prairie wind,
Now the bright stars lead me
To do His will,
Praise God,
Amen."

* * *

"Sergeant, can't you stop that chatter?
Beckwourth, what's the matter?
Can't you find the trail?"
"Does that half-breed know what he's doing?"
Splash, splash, through shallow water,
Lead horses breaking the thin ice.
"Goddamn! it's cold!"
"What d'ya suppose that half-breed's up to?"
"Who is it, Bent?"
"Yeah, old Bent's son, Robert."
"Suppose he led us in this lake
To get our powder wet?"
"Wouldn't put it past him.
Heard him tell old Beckwourth
He thought his brother Charley was with Black Kettle."
"Never trust a half-breed."
"You know old Beckwourth's half nigger,
So here we are led by them two,
Half-way to God's ass-hole!"
"I'm sleepy. Damn near fell off."
"Eat some hard-tack, that'll keep you awake."
"Tack weevils will, you mean."
Oh hard crackers, come again no more.
Cold. Hands cold, faces cold,
Sabers cold, carbines cold, rifles cold.
Steady ride on over short prairie grass,
Snow patches gleam, jeweled skies.

* * *

In his lodge on Sand Creek
White Antelope turns in his sleep.
He dreams of the Great White Father,
Seen years ago in Washington.
The clack, clack, clack of the Iron Horse,
The whistle shrieking and that steam and smoke,
With Little Chief and Alights-on-the-Cloud,
Riding to Washington on the iron rails.
The land went on forever.
The lodges of the Whites filled the land.
White faces staring, laughing;
White faces, white faces,
More white faces than the buffalo.
Little Chief was dead,
Alights-on-the-Cloud was dead,
Killed by the Pawnees.
Now the People huddled under the white wing
But the wing was squeezing them.
The Cheyenne were dying, smothered
By the white wing.
The white antelope stood in the snow,
Looked to the land of the ice,
To the land where the sun rises,
Looked to the warm lands always green,
Looked to the sun's home.
Around and around white wolves stand,
White snow swirls and down the great white bird
Descends, huge-winged.
It was the old dream,
The vision given him so long ago.
He feels the scars on his chest,
So long ago the drum beating,
And straining on the rope,
The peg tearing his flesh,
Straining for a vision,
Drums beating and
Straining for a vision
In the summer sun,

17

Sweating and staring for vision
Until it was cold,
The snow came down,
The drums were silent.
The snow came down.
He saw the white antelope,
White wolves,
White bird,
White snow.
White Antelope listens to the night,
Wind in the lodge poles,
Wind in the dry grass,
Wind over the patches of snow.
Lodge fire only a glow now,
A wolf howls, a dog barks.
White Antelope pulls the buffalo robe closer.
The Great White Father had given him a medal.
Black Kettle has a flag.
What medicine is this?
Sweet Medicine brought the arrows,
Long ago, long ago.
Now they are lost,
The Pawnees have them.
But what does it matter?
Sweet Medicine said the Whites would come,
White-faced men with hair on their faces
And we would all disappear.
Now we are camped under the White man's wing.

* * *

*Now, therefore, I, John Evans, governor of Colorado
Territory, do issue this my proclamation, authorizing
all citizens of Colorado, either individually or in
such parties as they may organize, to go in pursuit
of all hostile Indians on the plains, scrupulously
avoiding those who have responded to my said call
to rendezvous at the points indicated; also to kill
and destroy, as enemies of the country, wherever
they may be found, all such hostile Indians. And*

further . . . I hereby empower such citizens, or
parties of citizens, to take captive, and hold to
their own private use and benefit, all the property
of said hostile Indians that they may capture, and to
receive for all stolen property recovered from said
Indians such reward as may be deemed proper and
just therefore.

So Evans August 11, 1864, with a pistol on his hip,
"The conflict is upon us."
Imagined smoke in the clear blue air.
The wires hum to Washington and Leavenworth.
Herewith authorized . . . the usual forms,
Orders, the recruitment of one-hundred day volunteers,
Sound of hammering, up go the posters,
Wanted Indian Fighters.
Miners idling by the Montana Theater in Central City,
"Why not, hell.
Like to get me a red-skin."
"The mine's sure slow. I could use a ride.
Cap'n Sayr's all right. Let's go."

II. Fort Lyon & Camp Weld

The red sandstone rectangle of Fort Lyon
Breaks the slow roll of the prairie.
The white man's geometry, order, control.
Outside the walls the looser cones,
Buffalo-hide lodges, Cheyenne, Arapahoe,
Being pulled in; the walls will absorb them.
Whiskey, gunpowder, blankets, kettles, whiskey
For the buffalo skins, the last hunts,
Dust rising, the great herd, prairie wave,
Roar of hoofs, the great beasts
Driven, cut off, cornered by the fast ponies,
The shrill cries of the hunters
Last glimpse of Asia, the hunter,
The nomad driving the spear deep,
"Yip, yip, yip," the cries of the hunt,
Changeless under the sun.

The hides, sinews, thews, bones,
The man and the buffalo, the two,
Together, under the sun.
The medicine of the buffalo skull,
The hollow eyes watching.
The women, scraping, stretching, curing the skins,
The fine camp days after the hunt,
Days going back as long as one remembered.
Now the circle was broken.
Only the robes mattered,
Becoming whiskey, gunpowder, blankets, kettles, whiskey
And when the robes were gone,
Women becoming whiskey, gunpowder, blankets, kettles, whiskey.

* * *

Dust, dirt floors, baked parade ground,
Dry prairie dust, hot September breeze.
The prairie is brown, burnt.
Only the cottonwoods are green,
Marking the line of the Arkansas,
Low, but cool, still remembering the high mountains.
Major Edward Wynkoop, officer commanding, Fort Lyon,
Had his orders, clear, neat and precise,
Kill them, as that is the only way. —Chivington.
Repair the fort, drill the troops,
Send out patrols, keep busy.
Heat waves shimmer over the prairie,
Edgy, everyone;
Dust, smoke in the distance.
Cramer and Baldwin out after Arapahoes,
Wounded four and took a pony,
But the goddamned Starr carbines jammed.

Old Aunt Eliza, nobody's slave now,
Smiling, teasing Mrs. Snyder,
"You all got a mighty fine head of hair
For the Injuns to get, Honey."
Captain Gray found the government wagon,
The scattered household goods,

The bodies, two men, shot and scalped,
Dead wheel mule.
Flies buzz, swirl on the neat scalped skull,
Eyes blank to the sun.
"Burial party, Corporal."
Scattered contents of a sewing box, a dress, a shoe.
Wynkoop informs Chivington:

> My intention is to kill all Indians I may come
> across until I receive orders to the contrary
> from headquarters.

In Washington clerks have almost filed Spotsylvania
And turn now to Cold Harbor;
Grant lost 7,000 men in a half an hour,
But the clerks will soothe the grief with paper.
And even here at the edge of the Union,
Edge of time, on this prairie,
Where only now the ticking clocks begin to measure out the wind,
Even here, where then and now
Grate together like the hidden shifting plates,
Shelves of earth crust thrusting change,
Even here the papers soothe.
Wynkoop sits at his desk
Shuffling papers, feeling pleased
With their neat abstractions,
The reason of requisitions, the order of orders.
Here, at this edge of time,
Ploughs tear the prairie sod,
The buffalo carcasses rot in the sun,
Traders grin with beads, kettles, whiskey,
And wives turn whore to make braves drunk.
No wonder in this smoke and roar
Of civilizations edge to edge
Wynkoop admires the clarity and neatness of orders,
Comfort of abstraction,
And the precision of extermination.
"Goddamn it, Sergeant, I told you to kill Indians,
Not bring them to me."
"Well, Sir, he was waving this letter
And making all these peace signs,
So we brought him in."

One-Eye and Min-im-mie, Cheyenne braves,
Refusing to be abstractions,
Interfering with paperwork,
Objecting to Manifest Destiny and the course of civilization,
Imagining there was a choice,
That somehow we would not turn off I-25
For a hamburger
Or because the waters of Cherry Creek were cold and bright
And wild cherry grew rich along the banks
And the women would pound the cherries into the meat,
Preparing for winter,
Thinking because the land was sweet and good
That calendar, clock, file cabinet, computer
Would never sit on the banks of Cherry Creek
To turn its waters black and foul.
Anyway, there they were,
Extending the talking paper Bent wrote for them,
Refusing to be abstractions,
Silent, patient, sweaty after a long ride.
The chance of arrival was slight,
More likely a notch in a trooper's carbine,
An item in the daily report,
And dinner for the coyotes.
"Weren't you afraid you'd be killed?"
Asks Wynkoop, a man capable of surprise.
The steady voice, the rise and fall of strange, wild syllables,
The interpreter's halting twang,
He recalled years later and wrote it down,
As he remembered, a little florid and bookish,
But still filled with wonder at it,
What One-Eye said in that little room:

> *I am young no longer, I have been a Warrior, I have*
> *not been afraid to die when I was young, why should*
> *I be when I am old, therefore the Great Spirit*
> *whispered to me and said: 'You must try to save*
> *your people.'*

And Major Wynkoop, pioneer, City Father,
Whose street runs past Union Station in Denver,
Where Susan Ashley recalled the campfires of Cheyenne
Celebrating five Ute scalps,

The wild dance in the flickering light,
Wynkoop, even understanding the inevitability of that street:

> *I was bewildered with an exhibition of such patriotism*
> *on the part of two such savages, and felt myself in*
> *the presence of superior beings . . .*

And reads the letter from Black Kettle and others
Asking for talks, asking for peace,
And because One-Eye and Min-im-mie stood there,
In the hot little room, among the white papers,
No longer abstractions but themselves, One-Eye and Min-im-mie,
Wynkoop sets out one hundred forty miles
To meet Black Kettle.
Across the prairie, one hundred and twenty-seven men,
Two howitzers, ride towards the Smoky Hill,
Where two thousand Cheyenne and Arapahoe are camped.
Almost an exchange, enough at least,
For them both, One-Eye and Wynkoop,
To know something shared.
Riding through the fire, Black Kettle saw that,
Saw that sharing, those brave men, *riding through the fire.*
But still it was all talk,
Talk before the avalanche,
The small voices in the valley, talking,
Hoping somehow to persuade the avalanche not to come,
Hoping by words, charms, and magic
To stop the white fall,
The great rush, the roar of snows settling,
Yielding to their own weight,
Words suggesting the river should not flood,
The hurricane should not blow,
The mountains not rise,
Migrations not meet,
That somehow the Stone Age might survive
The steel rails,
Bark of carbine,
Howitzers tossing grape shot,
Completion of the circle,
Migration of gunpowder.
So Wynkoop, Si Soule, Cramer, and Phillips
Sit there in willow shade

By the north fork of the Smoky Hill
Listening as Smith and George Bent translate
The long speeches, the eloquence and anger.
The smoke of tobacco and willow bark rises
But peace is wispy, fleeting as the smoke.
Bull Bear is angry, distrustful,
"The Whites will always lie."
One-Eye, White Antelope, Heaps-of-Buffalo, Black Kettle,
Argue, cajole, pushing the anger down.
All around the surge and bustle of the Indian camp,
Six hundred warriors, restless, thinking of their power.
Lieutenant Hardin, nervous by the guns,
Holds the picket lines
While the council argues on.
The braves, curious, testing, jostle the white soldiers.
Black Bear laughs, pushes a grape in the howitzer's vent,
Shoulders the gunner, hoping for a fight.
But Black Kettle has seen the white lodges,
Knows the Whites are numerous as the grass.
Bull Bear cannot understand;
For him, for the young warriors,
The prairie ends only with the Shining Mountains,
Home of the Utes, the mountain people.
The land is vast,
The wind blows forever,
The buffalo will always darken the prairie.
Time is only this moment.
These Whites can easily die.
Bring in the white prisoners,
Wynkoop demands, *then I'll take you to the Chiefs in Denver,*
I am a little chief and can promise no more.
The talking is over.
The cavalry bivouacs twelve miles away.
Wait.
A bad night.
The usual noises.
Wind, wolves, sentry call.
Sawyer and a few others ready for mutiny.
Slow turn of the constellations,
"Corporal of the guard!"

Nothing, false alarm.
At last, morning and still waiting.
Noon and waiting.
Then the dust in the distance,
Resolves itself into riders.
First Left Hand with Laura Roper,
Then Black Kettle with three children.
Isabel Eubanks, four years old,
My little Golden-headed charge, Wynkoop wrote,
Daniel Marble and Ambrose Archer,
Both of them eight.
Ambrose said he'd just as soon
Stay with the Indians
But Laura Roper wept for joy,
Remembering the nights and the hard days
And Mrs. Snyder dead at the end of a calico rope.
But there are the prisoners,
A promise is kept.
Wynkoop holds his golden-headed charge,
Savoring the delicate beauty of the child,
Who would be dead in a year,
Dead before her mother would be recaptured,
And her owner, Two Face, hanged at Fort Laramie.
Now the little girl,
Warm in his arms,
Seems the sign of peace,
A pledge, a hope.
Wynkoop with a troop of forty cavalry;
Seven Indian chiefs and braves,
Black Kettle, White Antelope, Bull Bear, Cheyenne;
Neva, Bosse, Heaps-of-Buffalo, and No-ta-nee, Arapahoes;
Ride from Fort Lyon to Denver
To talk peace with the White Chief Evans, the governor.
The photograph shows dusty 14th Street;
Lawrence Street Methodist Church,
Where Chivington had preached;
Its bricklayer's Gothic, solid, formidable,
Unnatural in this emptiness;
A few clapboard cabins,
The Platte and its banks low in the background.

The wagons with the chiefs and captives in the foreground,
Behind them a straggle of carriages, twenty-five at least,
Come to see the spectacle.
Four or five men on horse, a few pedestrians
Scattered like extras complete the scene.
The shadows say it's just about noon.
There's a breeze as almost always.
It's a nice day.
Andy Stanbury, proprietor of the Tambien Saloon,
Leaving George to tend the bar,
Stares at the released captives and the goddamn Indians.
William Byers, editor of the *Rocky Mountain Daily News*,
Disappointed pro-statehood man, Chivington's good friend,
Looks on, too, "What's Wynkoop up to?"
The Indians seem dirty, wild, alien.
At a distance you might take them for squaws,
Wrapped in blankets, braids down their shoulders,
But the faces are hard, strong, and stern.
"Lo, the poor Indian," Byers spits in the dust.
"Let the Hundreddazers at those fellows, eh, Will?"
Andy Stanbury grins.
The Colorado boys, says Byers,
Will soon make the red devils howl!
"Look for that in the *News* tomorrow, Andy."
Black Kettle, tired and stiff from the cramped journey,
Stares at the church, new since he last came here,
To the white man's camp where the waters join.
No horse could pull it away,
No travois bear its weight.
The white man has come.
He will not go away.
He will cover the land with lodges of stone.
The People must make peace,
But the white men do not look kindly.

"Look, Major," the Governor says,
"What the hell can I do with the Colorado Third?
How can I make peace now?"
There it is. The weight of arms.
Already the taunts and jokes,

"The bloodless Third."
The bloodless Third, the Hundreddazers,
Need blood to take
Back to the wives and children,
Back to the mines,
Back to the saloons and whorehouses,
Back home to Central City, Boulder, Golden, Denver.
Blood for Washington,
Blood for politics,
Blood for the voters,
Blood to say,
"We did need the Colorado Third";
Blood for the record,
Blood for the books.
No one says where they stayed,
Black Kettle and the rest,
Waiting for the Governor to agree to talk.
Surely not the Planter's House on Blake Street,
With its "first class bar and billiard saloon"
And the "larder . . . supplied with the best the market affords."
So imagine them in a barracks room at Camp Weld,
Just another frontier post outside Denver
(Where now a cloverleaf joins U.S. 6 and Interstate 25).
At night they roll their blankets on the floor
And talk to hide the sentry tread, the white camp sounds.
White Antelope tells of Washington,
The steel road, the white lodges everywhere.
Bull Bear thinks that the white man dies like the Red.
Heaps-of-Buffalo tells a story of Wihio, the trickster.

* * *

Wihio was walking on the prairie,
Listening to the wind and watching a sparrow hawk
When he saw a strange man speaking to the stones,
Saying, "Turn over, stones,"
And the stones turned over,
"Turn over, stones"
And the stones turned over.
And Wihio said,

"Let me do that."
And the man said,
"You may do that;
It is easy to do that";
And the man showed Wihio the way.
"You see, Wihio,
It is easy,
You may do that;
It is easy to do that.
But you must remember,
You must remember, now,
You can do that four times only,
That you must remember now,
Four times only and no more."
And the man went away.
And Wihio said, "Roll over, stone!"
And the stone rolled over.
And Wihio said, "Roll over, stone!"
And the stone rolled over.
"Hey-a,hey-a, the stones rolled," Wihio cried,
And he danced.
"Hey-a, hey-a, the stones rolled over!"
Roll over, stone!
And the stone rolled over,
"Hey-a, hey-a, the stones rolled."
"Roll over, stone!"
And the stone rolled over.
"Hey-a, hey-a, the stones rolled over!"
And he danced.
"Roll over, stone!"
And the stone rolled right at Wihio
And Wihio ran
But the stone rolled faster
And rolled right onto Wihio.
And the stone sat on Wihio
And Wihio could not move.
And Wihio cried, "Oh, Father buffalo,
Come help me."
And the buffalo came
And he pushed hard at the stone,

But the stone was so big,
Yes, the stone was so big,
Even the buffalo could not move it.
He broke his horns,
The buffalo broke his horns.
Father Buffalo could not move it.
And Wihio cried to the Antelope,
But the Antelope could not move it.
And Wihio cried to brother Coyote,
But Coyote could not move it.
Oh, wise Coyote thought and thought,
But he could not move it.
None of the animals could move it,
And Wihio looked and looked
But there was no help.
Only way off,
High and way off,
A nighthawk flying.
And Wihio cried,
"Oh, little brother, listen,
Oh, little brother, listen.
I have a terrible thing to tell you.
This stone has said you are ugly,
This stone says you are an ugly bird,
This stone says you fly badly,
This stone says you hunt poorly,
This stone says your eyes are dull,
This stone says your beak is all crooked,
This stone says you are an ugly bird.
I said stop this, stone,
I said you're lying, stone,
But the stone got angry and rolled right on me.
You see how I am for telling the stone to stop these lies."
And the nighthawk flew up,
The nighthawk flew high up,
The nighthawk flew up until it was a little speck in the sky
And then flew down
And flew down and down
And hit the stone
With its beak,
Hit the stone,

With its beak,
Right in the middle,
And broke it in pieces.
And Wihio got up
And Wihio got up
And went to his lodge.

* * *

And then it seemed better in the wooden lodge of the White Man;
And they slept, waking only when the sentries changed,
And when the bugle told the White Man it was dawn.

Governor Evans is angry. Peace is not the plan.
Chivington is right.
Extermination is the only way.
They come in for the winter wanting peace,
Make war in summer and the prairie burns.
And what about the Third?
What about the bloodless Colorado Third?
Well, on with it.
Put on the Great White Father face
And listen, listen to this Black Kettle.

Black Kettle looks at the White Chief Governor
And at the White Soldier Chief called Chivington;
They say he is a brave chief
But his eyes are those of a mad buffalo.
John Smith will tell his words in English
And that man there will change his words to marks on paper.
That may not be good, but I must speak.
Wynkoop, Soule, and Cramer, he knows these white war chiefs.
I spoke to them at Smoky Hill.
They listened then; maybe these others will listen now:

> *I followed Major Wynkoop to Fort Lyon, and Major
> Wynkoop proposed that we come up to see you. We have
> come with our eyes shut, following his handful of
> men, like coming through the fire. All we ask is that
> we may have peace with the whites; we want to hold
> you by the hand. You are our father; we have been*

traveling through a cloud; the sky has been dark
ever since the war began. These braves who are with
me are willing to do what I say. We want to take
good tidings home to our people, that they may sleep
in peace. I want you to give all the chiefs of the
soldiers here to understand that we are for peace, and
that we have made peace, that we may not be mistaken
by them for enemies. I have not come with a little
wolf's bark, but have come to talk plain with you. We
must live near the buffalo or starve. When we came here
we came free, without any apprehension, to see you,
and when I go home and tell my people that I have taken
your hand and the hands of all the chiefs in Denver, they
will feel well, and so will all the different tribes of
Indians on the plains, after we have eaten and drunk with them.

Simon Whiteley's pen scratches away,
Amos Steck, the Denver lawyer, yawns.
What's the point of it all anyway?
The Indian's got to go.
But this one would make a good lawyer,
Windy enough anyway.
That one now, thought Chivington,
That's the one to watch, that big fellow, Bull Bear.
Imagine him with Laura Roper,
Or Mrs. Snyder, couldn't stand it, hanged herself.
Mrs. Eubanks still out there
In some filthy lodge
Driven to what in the darkness.
These savages will talk here
All Great-White-Father-Hold-Your-Hand
And rape and dance around their fires in a week.
Might even, who knows, to blond little Linda,
Stop at nothing, drawn to white skins.
Now Byers says in the *News*,
Heathen Chinese Rites In San Francisco.
Idolatry and lust on every side,
Burn incense and rape white girls on heathen altars.
My telegram to General Curtis at Leavenworth
Sets things straight:

Winter approaches. The Third Regiment is full, and they know they
will be chastised for their outrages and now want peace. I hope that
the major-general will direct that they make full restitution and then
go on their reserve and stay there.

—Chivington

Listen to that Bull Bear now;
"I am young, and can fight.
I have given my word to fight with the whites.
I am willing to die in the same way, and expect to do so."
You will, Bull Bear,
No matter what this old Chief Neva says now.
We'll see to that, Bull Bear.
No more white girls for you, Bull Bear,
Coyote dinner, Bull Bear,
Your scalp on my saddle bow, Bull Bear.
My turn to speak now; it's all over.
Time for me, the last words,
Firm and gentle and vague.
No promises and plenty of room to wiggle in.
Now I'll big-chief 'em.
Wish I'd worn my sword.

I am not a big war chief, but all the soldiers in
this country are at my command. My rule of fighting
white men or Indians is, to fight them until they
lay down their arms and submit to military authority.
You are nearer Major Wynkoop then any one else,
and you can go to him when you get ready to do that.

And somehow it was enough.
Black Kettle was pleased.
Handshakes all around.
Evans and Chivington smile, look wise,
Know something others don't.
Excuse themselves from the photograph
And its uneasy harmony.
Wynkoop and Soule kneel in front,
Benevolent, paternal,
Wynkoop's arm rests easily on One-Eye's knee.
They are young men, serious,

And look as if they believe they had arranged something,
Something real and true, not just another betrayal.
There, in the center, Black Kettle is calm,
His pipe of peace on his lap,
Just barely visible;
Wynkoop's service revolver forms a painterly vertical
Pointing to the pipe.
Oh, emblems are everywhere.
Flash! and the plate records the momentary blindness,
Eyes staring into the white light.
Photograph over, they all shake hands again,
Strange white gesture,
And disappear almost immediately
Into the archives,
Into attics and museums,
And the names of streets.
The unidentified man with the fine beard
And the gold watch fob,
All probity and self-possession,
Is he observant lawyer Steck,
Or the secretary, Whiteley, who wrote it down?
No matter, all long dead.
And the chiefs are dead now,
And John Smith, the interpreter,
Old Gray Blanket, with his Cheyenne wife,
Already there to meet them in '58,
When the miners came to Cherry Creek,
Tough old John, hawk-nosed wild man;
Beat his wife with a three-legged creepy,
Couldn't civilize old John.
Dead.
The soldier on the right,
Standing at sloppy attention,
Glad to be there with the officers and Indians,
Feeling important,
Glad to have his picture took,
Maybe a miner from Cripple Creek
Or a drover from Boulder,
A Hundreddazer waiting his time out,
With a story to tell in the saloon,

"Should'a seen them red-skins jump
When the powder went off,
Thought they'd shit buffalo chips."
Long dead.
Wynkoop and Soule, long dead.
But now they all look to the light,
The flash that hid for each
That last and private meeting.
One-Eye at Sand Creek,
Black Kettle four years later on the Washita,
And Soule's blood laying the dust of Lawrence Street
When Chivington's hired gun shot him down.
Now it's time to shake hands,
Touch the black box that makes lightning,
And then ride back to the prairie camp
And the warmth of familiar voices and fires,
Thinking that somehow there was peace
Now that they had taken the hands of the whites.
Back to Fort Lyon,
Believing that the White Man wanted peace too,
Believing that the Tall Chief, Wynkoop, would protect them,
That for a season only the winter and years would kill.

* * *

Wynkoop feeding the Indians at Fort Lyon.

DO NOT FEED THE INDIANS.
UNAUTHORIZED.
Telegraph clicks.
Relieved of command.

> *Special Orders No. 4,*
> *Major Scott J. Anthony*
> *Will proceed to and take command of Fort Lyon*
> *And will investigate and report upon*
> *Rumored issuance of stores, goods or supplies*
> *To hostile Indians in direct violation of orders.*
> *From the general commanding the department.*

DO NOT FEED THE INDIANS.

This Red-Eyed Chief is not their friend,
But still, here on the bend of Sand Creek,
They will be safe.
Here they are under the white man's arm.
Old Gray Blanket Smith is in camp,
Come to trade, come with a wagon
And two white soldiers from Red-Eyed Anthony.
Would Gray Blanket come if it were not safe,
Would Red-Eye send soldiers to a fire?
So the squaws can tend the camp,
The children run and play,
Cup-and-ball, roll the hoop, tops on the ice.
The winter days rise and fall,
The prairie is brown,
The willows are sleeping,
But the stories go round the lodge-fire at night
When the wind blows
And the Mistai squeak and hoot
In the dark, outside the firelight,
Outside the lodge-warmth, hide-warmth,
While the Seven Stars journey on.

* * *

They are brothers.
Seven brothers in the sky.
Seven brothers in the sky.
The girl brought them buckskin clothes,
Pretty girl brought them shirts and leggings.
Brought them moccasins and called them brothers.
They are brothers.
Seven brothers in the sky.
But the buffalo got angry.
Who knows why the buffalo got angry,
But they got angry,
The buffalo got angry.
They are brothers.
Seven brothers in the sky.
Buffalo chased them up the tree.
And the tree began to fall.

Tree began to fall.
So they cried to their little brother.
They are brothers.
Seven brothers in the sky.
Save us, brother.
So he shot an arrow far into the sky,
Shot an arrow far into the sky.
And the tree began to grow.
And the tree began to grow.
Way up, way up.
Grew way up.
Grew way up to the sky.
Grew way up to the sky
And they walked right off
Into the sky
And they walked right off
Into the sky.
They are brothers.
Seven brothers in the sky.

* * *

The sky domes over the village on Sand Creek.
The Seven Brothers move through the sky.
The children sleep warm in the tepees.
In their dreams they wonder about the girl
But no one can tell what happened to her.
Her brothers move through the sky.
Coyotes bay, fire falls,
Wind edges round the tepees,
The tethered ponies shuffle, stamp, and snort
At the sound of something far off.
Old Sparrow Hawk Woman gathering wood
In the almost dawn listens,
Far off, something, far off.
Coming near.

III. Sand Creek

Wind rises in the early dawn light.
Stars and Stripes flap and snap,
Color-Sergeant jerks awake from saddle-drowse.
Low talk ripples through the ranks,
Troops feeling the dawn,
Big Dipper under the horizon,
Stars dimming out,
First red just touching the east,
Feeling more awake and edgy,
The morning's work to come.
"Cold, boy?" laughs Corporal Whitelaw,
"Get you nice warm Indian pussy today, boy,
Nothing like Indian pussy to warm a man up,
Right, boy?"
"You, Whitelaw, pipe down!"
"Ah, Sarge, just talkin' about fuckin' and cuttin'
For instruction like for this here boy.
This here boy wouldn' hardly know what to do
If I didn't tell him.
Trainin' the troops, Sarge,
Just doin' my job."
"Shut up, Whitelaw,
You know the Colonel don't like that kind of talk."
"No, he don't like talk, Sarge,
But he'd like to nail a few squaws,
Just nail 'em down comfortable like,
Just like everybody else and maybe more.
And he sure like to get a little scalpin' after.
Oh, Colonel Chivington don't mind stickin' a squaw or so
Long as, after they's good and dead, good dead Indians after."
"You men, silence in ranks!"
Clank, click, rattle, metal on metal,
Soft squeak of leather on leather,
The plod and jangle of the troops
Over the now sandy turf.
"Regiment . . .
Battalion . . .
Company . . .

37

Squadron . . . halt!"
There in the white dawn light,
Here and there a few threads of smoke,
The night fires burned low,
The morning fires just being fed,
The white tepees glow,
Now tinged, each minute, more red
In the dawn's early light.
Some hundred lodges
There, on the bow bend of the creek,
By the willow stand,
The tents of the bands—
Sand Hill, Left Hand, Black Kettle,
Lone Bear, White Antelope, War Bonnet,
The village sleeping still
In the last glow of the red dawn.

"Now, men, there are the tents of Makkedah,
There the heathen ungodly,
Remember the blood on the plains of the Platte,"
Chivington, monumental on his horse,
The great voice rising,
"Remember your wives, your children, your loved ones.
Their blood stained the sands
And the river ran red.
Remember the rapes and the blood, boys,
Remember the cruel tortures, the rapes and the blood,
Remember the scalps and the fires, boys.
Boys, remember.
Serve God and bring us peace, remember.
And, boys, *Nits make lice,*
Remember!"

* * *

Now it begins.
Gray Squirrel Woman rushes to tepee flap
To meet a shot
Which hurls her back
Onto the buffalo robe bed,

Onto the baby.
And dies with the baby beneath her.
Gray Blanket Smith with Louderback and teamster Clark
Are in the village with a wagonload of trade goods,
It being a peaceful trading time,
These Indians at peace.
A good time for Smith to visit his Cheyenne wife
And his son, Jack, who lives between the worlds,
Jack, sometimes white, sometimes red.
Smith wakes to the shouts and carbine fire.
Rushes out to meet the troops with a white flag.

"Shoot the old son of a bitch,
He's no better than an Indian."
"Christ, Louderback, let's get out of here."
Now Black Kettle has the flag up,
The white man's stars and stripes,
Waving on the lodge pole,
The flag from Washington,
The Great White Father's flag,
Beneath it a white flag flutters.
"Now they will know we are peaceful,
The white man will not shoot now."

"Sonna bitch got a flag up,
Shoot the bastard."

Black Kettle knows now,
There is nothing but flight,
Calls to White Antelope to run,
But White Antelope stands still in the creek bed,
Sings calm in the creek bed,
Arms folded, sings his death song,
Nothing lives long,
Except the earth and the mountains.
Sings the old chant,
Sings the death song,
Sings.
"Got the old bastard!"
"Big Chief, that one."

"Nice silver brooch on that scalp lock.
Real fine rings on his fingers."
"Jesus, great big balls!"
"Gonna have a nice tobacco pouch there, boy,
Real nice sou-ven-ir, yessir!"
"Yahoo!"
Nothing lives long,
Except the earth and the mountains.
"Yahoo! Get that little sucker!"
Nits make lice.
"Yahoo!'
"Have a drink."
"Let's get that squaw!"
"Yahoo!"

* * *

All along the creek bed now
Puffs of smoke.
The Indian retreat has been slow,
Determined.
Those in rifle pits
Dug in the high sand bank to the northeast
Contest each step.
Fire until bullets or arrows are gone.
Die slowly, fiercely.

> *The Indians fought desperately, apparently resolved*
> *to die upon that ground, but to injure us as much*
> *as possible before being killed. We fought them*
> *for about six hours along the creek for five miles.*

The report of Major Anthony,
Who watched it all and found,
As massacres go,
It was a terrible one
And such a one as each of the hostile tribes
On the plains richly deserve.
Richly deserve.

Morse Coffin, Company D,

Farmed east of Longmont,
Remembered long hours behind a willow clump,
Or sometimes lying flat behind a drift of sand,
Firing at "some little dark object,
Which could now and then be seen."
The nature of war,
Mostly a fragment, vaguely seen.
Firing until his Smith and Wesson carbine jammed,
Coffin hadn't learned the soldiers' trick
To wet the shells in the mouth before loading,
That intimacy,
Which makes it easy to remove the cartridge after firing.
He and another fellow from the Third,
Some other company, fellow with a Garibaldi musket,
Had an "awful bore" and made a hell of a racket,
Them both firing at that "little dark object
Which could now and then be seen,"
Firing for almost two hours,
Until the other fellow left to rejoin his company
And Morse Coffin's carbine jammed.
Going back next day, after the battle,
Found just a squaw and a papoose dead in the hiding place,
But beyond it, the brave they thought they'd hit,
Was dead and scalped, too.
Well, someone saved Coffin "that trouble."
Bits and pieces.
Fragments.
Judge Ripley's hat shot off,
Or so they said. Coffin wasn't sure.
Perhaps the wind took it
As the old judge galloped in pursuit
Of some fleeing brave,
Or rode towards the rifle pits
And those deadly puffs of smoke.
"Lost my damn hat,"
Just barely noticed,
But something that became larger,
A fragment that became part of the definition,
And the collective memory,
Sand Creek and Judge Ripley's hat,

In summer chats in Longmont
When the farmers came in to market
And remembered.
Nothing really surprising.
The oddments of the historical catalogue,
Judge Ripley's hat and documented bits of flesh.
Morse Coffin produced MacFarland's chest ripped open,
His broken Smith & Wesson crammed in it,
They thought his heart was torn out,
It wasn't.
The surgeon found it later.
But the Indian's heart,
The unnamed Indian, not listed in the records,
Who sang or shouted, Coffin says,
All the time he fought,
Till Phillips and Lockhart finally killed him,
His heart was there,
Hanging on a bush.
Make it a willow.
Heart, bright, fresh, in the winter sun.
Chivington went out with Smith
To count the bodies.
"Who was that, John,
Do you think?"
But he's too torn,
Too torn for naming.
Scalps were going for ten dollars each,
Ten dollars each in Denver,
Good money in 1864.
Bodies in the creek bed,
Bodies in the rifle pits,
Bodies on the bluff,
Bodies scattered here and there.
It was over by three in the afternoon
And you could count the corpses
In the late winter sun:
White Antelope, Standing Water, One-Eye,
Scalped and cut;
War Bonnet, Spotted Crow, Two Thighs,

Scalped and cut;
Bear Man, Yellow Shield, and Yellow Wolf,
Scalped and cut.
What is this child's name?
Scalped and cut.
Was it Prairie Flower Morse Coffin shot
Out of pity because she was so painfully dying?
Was it Little White Fox Woman who lay still beside her,
Was it she Cox shot and scalped when she sat up dazed?
Was it she?
Fragments.
Bits and pieces of the day.
Shy Elk Woman
Held there in Black Kettle's tent,
Most of the afternoon.
Nothing for history,
Even for our memory.
Pain everywhere.
Whiskey smell.
Weight.
Tear.
The baby is dead.
Nothing new.
"Look Senator, that's how armies are."
Any Senator, any Senate,
Any army, any time.
"Gettin' some good fuckin', boy,
And a little cuttin'?"
"Yahoo! Jesus, oh, boy!"
"Lookit that, fella'
Lookit that."
"Yahoo! Jesus, oh, boy!
Never did cut me out a cunt before!
Gonna make me a real nice hat band, uh boy?"
"Boy, you take a bit of Indian cunt
And let it dry on your saddle bow,
Keep stretching it with your hand,
Gotta keep working it, boy,
Treat it just like beaver skin
And get yourself a real nice hat band."

"Yeah!"

*All manner of depredations were inflicted on their persons;
they were scalped, their brains knocked out; the men used
their knives; ripped open women, clubbed little children,
knocked them in the head with their guns, beat their
brains out, mutilated their bodies in every sense of
the word.*

—John S. Smith, Interpreter

*I did not see a body of man, woman, or child but was scalped,
and many in the most horrible manner--men, women, and
children's privates cut out; I heard one man say he
had cut out a woman's private parts and had them for
exhibition on a stick; I heard another man say that he
had cut the fingers off an Indian to get the rings on
the hand . . .*

—James D. Cannon, First Lieutenant,
First Infantry, New Mexico Volunteers

*The papoose was carried in a feed-box of a wagon a
day or a day and a half, and then it was thrown out and
left in the road; I do not know whether they killed it or
not.*

—David Louderback, Private,
First Colorado Cavalry

*I do not think I saw any one but what was scalped; saw
fingers cut off, saw bodies with privates cut off, women
as well as men. I saw Major Sayre, of the 3d regiment, scalp
an Indian for the scalp lock ornamented by silver ornaments:
he cut off the skin with it.*

—Lucien Palmer, Co.C,
First Colorado Cavalry

*I saw but one woman who had been killed, and one who had
hanged herself; I saw no dead children.*

—John M. Chivington, formerly Colonel,
First Colorado Cavalry

44

*I saw one or two men who were in the act of scalping, but
I am not positive.*

> —George L. Shoup, formerly Colonel
> Third Regiment Colorado Cavalry

Far off, the voices dim and distant now.
Dusty voices in Report on the Conduct of the War, 38th Congress,
Dusty voices in Senate Executive Document 26, 39th Congress,
Dusty voices in Reports of the Committees, 39th Congress.
Now, it is all long ago.
The newspapers are brittle,
Crumble to dust in the hands.
The microfilm reader makes a soft, sighing sound,
Dusty voices in long dead winds.
It was a long ride,
A hard ride.
Nits make lice.
Remember the murdered women and children on the Platte.
Lots of whiskey.
All that.

* * *

Wise Elk, five arrows left,
Waits beneath a buffalo robe
Until the whites are close.
Ya-ee, there is one, fires,
And fires three more before he's killed.
Singing all the time.
What did he sing?
What did he sing?
It was over in the afternoon.
Time for quiet scalping,
Gang rape,
And resting in the sun,
Smoking and talking, tired.
Time to shoot old John Smith's half-breed son.
"Colonel, they're goin' to shoot Jack Smith."
"I said, no prisoners. I have no orders to give."
"Some of the boys dragged the body

Out onto the prairie,
And hauled it about
For a considerable time."
The campfires, cold night,
The long wait for dawn,
Dogs barking all the time,
And fear outside the ring of light.
Pickets firing at shadows,
Cree's voice, "Fall in, Third Battalion,"
Nichols' echo, "Fall in, Company D,"
Tumble out of blankets to stare at the shadows in the night,
Then back to twitching sleep,
The howling dogs and slow turn of stars.
And by twos and threes,
The small bands, the remnants,
Moving slowly through the night,
Nursing wounds, pausing only for death,
And then moving slowly on, slowly,
To the camp of the People on Smoky Hill River,
The remnants, the survivors.
Black Kettle with his wife, Medicine Woman Later,
Bloody, nine wounds in her body when they could count,
Left Hand with his leg broken,
Making their slow way
To the camp of the People.

IV. And After

Home.
Lost.
The prairie shrinking every day.
The hunt smaller, smaller.
Buffalo carcasses stripped,
Rotting in the sun.
The iron rails
Binding the earth
And always the whites
With their ploughs,
Schools, and guns.

The last act.
Garryowen sounds on the Washita
Where Black Kettle dies.
Over and over *Garryowen* sounds.
Play *Garryowen* boys
For a white scalp dance.
"Over a hundred scalps!
How about that!"
Apollo Theater in Denver rocks with cheers,
"Yahoo for the Colorado Third,
Yahoo for the Bloody Third!"
But the bloody scalps
Even in Denver City in 1865
Finally offend,
Look out of place,
In a curtained parlor,
Shocking on the rosewood Chickering
Which brought Boston to the mountains' edge.
Letters are written.
Committees are formed.
The Senate, the House will investigate.
And God deliver us from such fools
As you down-easters,
Prays Byers in the *News.*
But the gavel bangs anyway.
Bang! In session.
Bang! That sounded like a shot.
It was.
Someone didn't want Si Soule to testify.
So a man named Squiers shot him dead on Lawrence Street.
One of those good western scenes.
They meet and fire, Soule falls.
Zoom in for a close-up,
Bullet through the head,
Blood spreading on the thirsty dust.
Then follows the chase.
Lieutenant Cannon caught Squiers in New Mexico
And brought him back.
Too bad for Jim Cannon.
"Cannon, Lieutenant Cannon, you awake?"

Calls Mack, clerk at the Tremont House.
No answer.
When they got the door open,
Mrs. Paul, a boarder there,
Peered through the door and saw him,
Dead, slumped in his chair,
Sun catching the dust motes
In the window light,
Soft breeze stirring the curtains,
A wagon passing outside.
Dead.
Mrs. Paul, bold, entered,
Touched his forehead, found it still warm,
Thought him an hour dead.
A. J. Randall testified he'd seen him drinking,
Gambling at the Progressive and Diana saloons.
A packet of morphia found in the room;
Some said he was poisoned.
But nobody knows.
A minor mystery.
Coroner's jury found,
"Death from congestion of the brain."
Not much to film here,
Just easing the body down the backstairs,
Hardly even an hotelier's embarrassment
In the Tremont House in Denver in 1865.
Squiers somehow escaped again,
Just gone in the night.
A rotten epilogue.

> *As to Colonel Chivington, your committee can*
> *hardly find fitting terms to describe his conduct.*
> *Wearing the uniform of the United States, which*
> *should be an emblem of justice and humanity . . . .*
> *Having full knowledge of their friendly character, having*
> *himself been instrumental to some extent in placing*
> *them in their position of fancied security, he*
> *took advantage of their inapprehension and defenseless*
> *condition to gratify the worst passions that ever*
> *cursed the heart of man . . .*

The rhetoric of the nineteenth century,
Rich, Congressional, flowed on,
But Chivington's commission was long expired,
Court-martial out of the question,
No final drama there.
Chivington drifted around and dwindled.
Freighting in Nebraska,
Editing the *Press* in Blanchester, Ohio,
Ran for the Ohio legislature,
But someone remembered Sand Creek
And he came back to Denver,
Still protesting,
"I stand by Sand Creek."
Maybe one last look, 1883,
A celebration for the Denver Pike's Peak Pioneers,
Lovely day, band plays "Garryowen,"
Enthusiasitic applause, then ruddy and portly,
Gray now, but still the preacher's booming voice,
Big John Chivington,
What of that Indian blanket that was captured
Fringed with white women's scalps?
I say here . . . I stand by Sand Creek.
1892, the big funeral for the hero.
Masons in the center,
Grand Army of the Republic on the right,
Over there, to the left,
The Colorado Pioneers' Association
And the Pioneer Ladies' Society.
The Reverend McIntyre preached.

* * *

Drive east on Colorado 96,
A hundred miles from Pueblo,
Used to be a steel town, raw-edged on the Arkansas,
Through the little prairie villages,
Not much more than names on the map,
Boone, Olney Springs, Ordway, Sugar City,
Across Horse Creek, Adobe Creek,
Mostly always dry, just sandy beds asking for water,

Through Haswell, Galatea, Eads, finally Chivington.
There in the prairie nowhere,
His name remembered.
It was once a tiny railroad town;
Now there's just an abandoned school,
With the wind moaning in its broken windows,
Completely desolate if it weren't for the bright sky
And the brown undulation of the prairie.
Drive through Chivington to the county road,
North across the Missouri-Pacific Railroad tracks
To the sign which points the way to the battlefield.
Better to leave the car here
And walk up the sandy track
To the granite marker,
"Site of Sand Creek Battle, November 29, 1864."
The creek bed is dry.
The bend larger than it was
By a hundred years of springtime floods
Which hurl the brush against the willow stand.
Cattle graze where the lodges stood.
My presence spooks them;
And they move off west,
Towards the high ridge
Where the ponies were tethered.
Nothing to see really.
The prairie, the sky, a circling hawk.
I'd hoped for ghosts,
Or even just a souvenir,
An arrowhead, a bit of rusted spur,
Some sign.
Nothing.
Only the wind blows.
The wind.
Nothing.
A song.
Nothing lives long
Except the earth and the mountains.
A song.
"That cuts it off."

Two Epilogues
At the Site of the Sand Creek Massacre

Just as we arrive a hawk buckles,
Gyres up and off,
Breaking the blue with its fierce wings.
Unseen, some small creature scurries off,
Saved by this chance crossing of lives.
We sit in the willow stand, listening
To voices.
Wind in the leaves, bird calls,
Distant cattle talk,
And White Antelope singing his death song,
Nothing lives long
But the earth and the sky.
An oriole flashes in the willows,
Completing the signs.

Note Found in an Old Box

An old, box, wooden,
Stain-faded and scratched.
Hidden away in the attic, forgotten.
Containing —well,
Some withered, dried thing
And a scrap of yellowed paper,
On it in faded ink, neat hand,
Ear from Sand Creek—
November 29, 1864—
I don't know why I did that.

ABOUT THE AUTHOR

Charles Squier was born in 1931 in Milwaukee and grew up in Shorewood, Wisconsin, within sight and sound of Lake Michigan. His mother's stories of Indians who visited his grandfather's farm in Michigan, of the stone tools, arrowheads, and other objects his plow turned up in the fields and her accounts of French Canadian voyageur ancestors gave him an early awareness of Native American history. He did his undergraduate work at Harvard, served in the U.S. Army at the end of the Korean War, returned to Harvard for a Master of Arts in Teaching. He received a PhD from the University of Michigan in 1963 and joined the faculty of the English Department of the University of Colorado where he taught courses in Shakespeare and Renaissance literature. His interest in travel was enhanced by stints as a visiting professor at the University of Liverpool, England; Université Paul Valéry in Montpellier, France; and at the Tianjin Foreign Language Institute in Tianjin, People's Republic of China. He retired from the University of Colorado in 1999. He has enjoyed acting in a variety of local dramatic productions and is a member of the Colorado Shakespeare Oratorio Society.